THE TRUE STORY OF
OLIVER BROWN
THE HEDGEHOG

ELAINE DREWERY

Published July, 2014
Printed by TSW Printers, Scunthorpe, North Lincs DN15 7NW

Text and Illustrations
©
ELAINE DREWERY

ISBN 0 9514810 1 0

All rights reserved. No part of this publication maybe reproduced, stored in a retrieval system or be transmitted in any form or by any means, electronic, mechanical, photo-copying, recording or otherwise without the prior written consent of the publisher.

THE TRUE STORY OF
OLIVER BROWN THE HEDGEHOG

A happy young hedgehog had spent the night enjoying a two mile forage through Hazel Nut Wood, deep in the heart of Lincolnshire. Because he was nocturnal, morning light warned him that he should hasten home to his leafy heap in a hedge near Hogsthorpe. He had eaten lots of bugs and beetles, slugs and snails and he burped and smiled at his round full tummy. He yawned as he turned by the blackthorn bush towards the lane, too dozy to worry about the noise of speeding traffic. All he wanted was to sleep away the daylight. He was so tired. His fat little feet pattered across the tarmac until suddenly he realised a black wheeled monster, fast and threatening was rumbling towards him. Fearfully he rolled up and prickled his spines in every direction to protect himself as nature had dictated for millions of years. He felt a fierce pain in his head, sailed through the air and knew no more.

Mrs. Brown drove carefully down the country lane and dutifully stopped when she came to a little hedgehog lying in a pool of blood. Cautiously she looked closer. Tentatively she picked him up and laid him gently on the grass at the side of the road before driving on to do the shopping. She hoped the little hedgehog would be all right, he wasn't very old and it was sad to think of him being hurt. It would be dreadful if that one picked himself up and

he burped and smiled at his round full tummy

wandered back into the road again. Her worries multiplied and magnified until she realised that her shopping wasn't so important. She turned her car round and sped back to rescue the hedgehog. He was just where she had left him and he looked seriously ill. Carefully she gathered him up, wrapped him in her cardigan, sank him into the soft comfort of a cushion on the back seat and rushed him to the hedgehog hospital at Authorpe near Louth.

Hedgehog Care offered nursing for weak, sick and injured hedgehogs. His head injuries were so severe that there seemed little hope of recovery. But after his wounds were gently bathed, he was pillowed on a bag of ice and left in the recovery position, safe from noise and light. Worried whispers and shaking heads hovered over him all day and night. He was so battered, so hurt, so still. There were several tears shed on him and quite a lot of prayers said over him.

Early one morning he woke up and wondered wherever he was. His head hurt and he was hungry. There was a dish of food nearby. He blinked his eyes and wondered why he felt all frosty round the face. He wanted to eat but his legs were numb and heavy. When he tried to move forward he slipped back. He was so confused. He heaved and hoisted and fell headlong in the dinner. He gobbled and guzzled and slurped and wondered what it was he had eaten. He couldn't move away from the dish so he was glad when someone lifted him clear. He could hear how surprised and pleased they were that he was alive. His face was cleaned, his head was smoothed and he was placed the right way up. He fought his way back to the food again. His legs were awkward and he couldn't stand but he ate more whilst he was supported by hands. He felt like eating for ever, he wanted more and more. He heard them call him Oliver Brown and say that he was brain damaged.

It was a miracle that Oliver Brown survived his head injuries having been unconscious at Hedgehog Care for three days. His determination to live had touched the hearts of everyone who had seen him. Now he was to be patiently worked upon to help him sort out his confusion and try to walk again. Lovingly he was guided and supported and encouraged to stand firmly on his faltering feet. He had a lot to learn and would have many difficulties.

He didn't remember that humans should be avoided. Here they provided cat food in a dish from a tin. When he fell they picked him up. When he wobbled they steered him forward and held him steady. They cheered the chills from his bruised body with comforting hot water bottles wrapped in towels. They snuggled him into a warm woolly blanket when he was tired of the light and needed to sleep in his leafy heap in a hedge that he couldn't find anymore. When his head wasn't hurting too much he tried hard to think but thoughts wouldn't come because he couldn't remember the things that his muddled memory had made him forget. His head didn't hurt as often as it had done because it was healing well and humans were helping to keep him happy in hospital. He was clean and comfortable.

Generally he responded to his therapy and grew stronger. There was great rejoicing the day he was able to frown his skin of prickles over his head and bottom like a huge blanket, then tighten it up with his muscles to pull himself into a prickly ball. Safely curled up he peeped cutely at his nurses through his fingers. He looked much better now.

Again and again he heard explained to people who asked "Why is he called Oliver Brown?". "Mrs. Brown rescued him and he always wants more food like Oliver Twist". Oliver Brown had no idea who Mrs. Brown was; knew nothing of his accident and even less about Oliver Twist. He was annoyed but not frightened by pink human fingers that held and tended him, so every now and then he bit them to preserve his dignity. It was the only way he felt he could assert himself and made him feel much better.

In one of the rows of hospital cages was a pretty lady hedgehog called Silly Jilly. Rescued from a tank on an industrial estate, she had been caked in a strong smelly chemical that had set like a shell around her. It had to be chipped off then the remainder soaked and brushed away. She suffered convulsions for nearly two weeks and was expected to die from the strain on her heart. However,

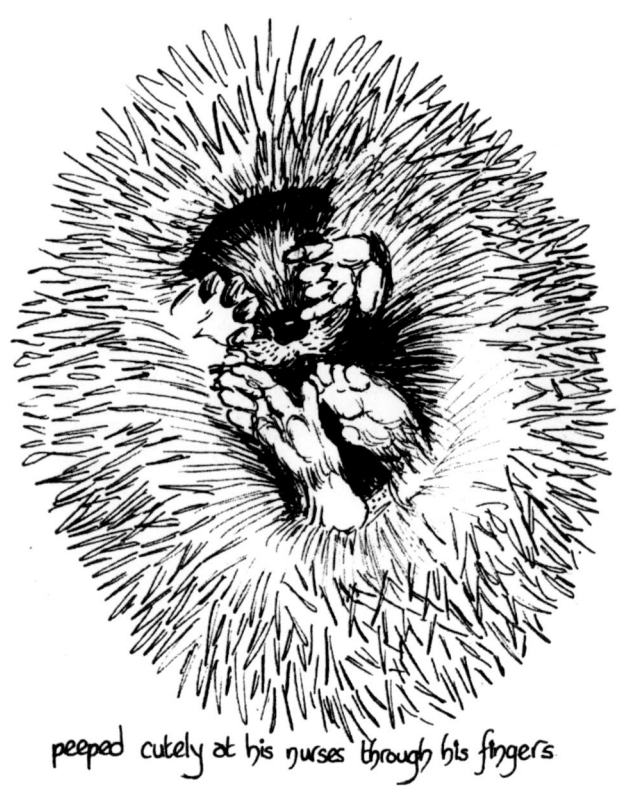

peeped cutely at his nurses through his fingers.

constant smoothing words, cuddles and love helped her to relax until happily she recovered. Every morning she climbed defiantly out of her cage to be discovered in the chosen company of the nearest gentleman hedgehog. She was blonde, beautiful and a shameless flirt who inspired an idea to help Oliver Brown.

Romance for hedgehogs is a complicated affair and courting couples have to be very careful. To make sure that his lady falls obligingly in love, the male hedgehog has to encircle her for as long as she crouches, watching him constantly, frigid, prickly and shy. Quite determined he patiently puffs round and round until he reveals to her how irresistibly handsome he is as she peeps coyly at him through her prickles. Gradually she has to admit what a wonderful partner he would make, so she lowers her prickles and lets them fall into a smooth coat which makes her really nice to be near. Cuddly and loving, the couple then make arrangements about having a family.

No one can explain all this to a hedgehog, nature has to take its course to make things happen by instinct and this was hopefully what would persuade Oliver Brown to take to his feet and with a true purpose, walk unassisted.

Looking radiantly beautiful, Silly Jilly was positioned on the kitchen floor and was impressed with the handsome fellow facing her even though he looked drunk. Oliver Brown tippled sideways then realised he wasn't alone. His shiny black nose waffled and twitched as he flushed with excitement and stood on his toes. He wanted to dance for joy he felt so happy. Ring o' Roses! She was the loveliest thing he had ever seen. He lurched forward to have a better look. Twisting and turning he moved about, balancing lightly without assistance. He was moving, he felt wonderful, he was in love! Faster and faster he twinkled his toes. Round and round thinking of nothing but Silly Jilly.

She stared and stared and started to giggle. He hadn't gone anywhere but was pivoting on the same piece of floor like a spinning top. He was a funny fellow. Oliver Brown closed his eyes as he dreamed of love and danced on. Silly Jilly threw back her head and laughed and laughed and rolled about with mirth. This fellow was a clown. Suddenly she noticed a box near the oven and saw a black hedgehog inside. Pawson's injured leg was completely better and he sat surveying the scene, looking serious, strong and sensible. Her heart fluttered and quickly she rolled onto her feet and scuttled eagerly into his box. They fell in love immediately and promptly made arrangement for having a family.

Oliver Brown hadn't noticed because he was still spinning his happy love dance. On and on he twirled until, breathless and dizzy, he stopped and gasped in disappointment. She had gone, it had all been a dream. He was confused, angry, hungry. He tippled sideways and forgot which foot to use to balance. Pink fingers steadied

Silly Jilly threw back her head and laughed and laughed

him and a dish of food was placed nearby. He tottered forward and ate whatever it was. He felt lost and funny and sad. He burped and wandered wearily to a corner. Oliver Brown had walked.

There are about one hundred hedgehogs at a time hoping to recover at Hedgehog Care. The aim is to return patients as soon as possible to the territory from which they have been taken. Obviously if one has been snatched from the jaws of an over indulgent Jack Russell he will be rehomed elsewhere, as will the ones rescued from notoriously vandalised public parks and sports fields, or the ones bordered by boundary lines of motorways, dual carriageways, bypasses and other environmental hazards.

New arrivals quarantined in cardboard boxes in the kitchen are named, labelled and stacked in high-rise flats whilst the sad little casualties are assessed and diagnosed. Special care is taken to isolate patients suffering from skin rashes or tummy upsets as these problems can easily spread to others. They are comforted with a hot water bottle wrapped in a towel, and covered with a woolly blanket. Routine treatment for fleas and worms is given appropriately, medication administered to those in need and those requiring surgery are rushed to the vet.

* * *

After the freedom of the Great Outside, confinement

to a cardboard box, in spite of its luxury and safety, can be claustrophobic torture to a wild animal. Expert observation soon recognises that an energetic patient hustling and scratching to get out is not glowing with athletic health but in a state of panic that could prove fatal. Additional space or a companion or sometimes a sympathetic human cuddle might answer the desperate plight of a hurt and frightened hedgehog. Some can only be pacified by a snug cradle in a bra or polo neck, which is why devoted hedgehog nurses often have body lumps in the most unexpected places.

The bathroom provides a recovery area where a patient is encouraged to explore through the opening in his box. As pneumonia is a threat to the bedridden after an operation, mobility and social life is there for the taking between the intensive nursing and horrific injuries. Though it is heartrending and humbling to watch these handicapped hedgehogs struggling to survive it is also an absolute inspiration. There are three-legged heroes adapting to amputation, stiff walking shuffles with shattered limbs pinned in place and hop-along hedgies heaving heavy plasters as they clump around the lino. Nerve wrecked chemically poisoned patients tremble and tumble uncontrollably amongst wired up casualties with broken jaws trying to uphold dignity while they wonder why life has become so frustrating. There is no better place to appreciate courage, or how precious life is than in this cluttered and messy bathroom – the 'après op ward'.

Recuperating hedgehogs are housed in rows of cages lining the front room. Grouped together where compatible they await their turn in outside rehabilitation runs to adapt to earth, elements and independence prior to release.

The ones too severely disabled for survival in the wild are either fostered out to enclosed gardens or given a welcome in the T.V. room. They choose their own little spot or bundle in a group either behind or inside the settee, under the stairs or in any of the many available boxes that litter the floor. By human standards hygiene is maybe questionable but those who object to the smell of hedgehogs are not particularly welcome anyway. Priority is for the invited residents, the ever increasing prickly handicapped house guests. It is homely and happy but bulging at the seams.

Those of suitable character join the Public Relations team for helping with talks and lectures at schools and organisations. Now that Oliver Brown could walk it was decided that association with other hedgehogs might prove to be helpful therapy. His abnormal behaviour was becoming increasingly apparent, so although it was unlikely that he would recover sufficiently for the wild he showed potential for becoming a member of the P.R. team. Here he would represent his species when he met the people who could learn to improve the world for future hedgehogs.

At dusk Oliver Brown, in a box, was situated in the T.V. room and was soon visited by several long stay hedgehogs with various responses. There was a degree of huffing and puffing, several puddles of excitement and a few strategically arranged 'poohs'. It was all about sorting out importance, boundaries and supremacy. Oliver Brown ignored it all, just ate his dinner as usual and looked upwards to see if any more was forthcoming. He was a large and truly handsome hedgehog as he emerged slowly from his box to begin circling crazily, bumping into unaccustomed objects in his confusion. His circles were alternated with straight dashes and abrupt stops as if he was about to hurry off somewhere then halted because he had forgotten his intention. Hope for improvement faded after weeks of similar relentless performance. It was now evident that dear Oliver Brown's severe head injuries had left him brain damaged. In his own little world he hurried about as if he was trying to catch up with time: always late. He only needed sanctuary to live out his years, he was no trouble, just one of God's creatures come to grief at the wheels of mankind. Well mannered and reserved amongst his own kind he was confident, slightly aggressive and deservedly resentful towards the humans that had caused his disability. He was much loved and admired by the hundreds of people to whom he was introduced, and treated with tentative respect by his handlers who had all at some time experienced a bite of discipline from the obtuse Oliver Brown.

Amongst the T.V. room residents who silently watched the arrival of Oliver Brown's box sat Rolly, the self-imposed company leader whose authority was never challenged. Although he was small, had a sideways snout and an eye and several toes missing, he swaggered and rolled about with an unmistakable air of bristling importance. It was generally assumed that his injuries had been acquired as a result of a raging battle, or an encounter with an articulated lorry. Confidentially it was nothing of the sort.

A gentleman had decided that a wall would take less maintenance than his ancient garden hedge, so he ordered a J.C.B. to uproot it. The menacing machine arrived for duty on the same day that a panting mother hedgehog gave birth to seven hoglets in a cozy nest between the gnarled roots of the hedge. She had hollowed out the earth, packed it with leaves, twigs and grass and a Mars bar wrapper; then circled, brushed and teaseled it all soft and fluffy with her prickles. Satisfied she delivered and tended her young. Then tired and full of pride, relaxed to feed them all. She didn't imagine as she dozed that the noise outside could possibly threaten her humble haven. Suddenly her peace was shattered, daylight glared with a deafening roar and her babies and lovingly built nest were tossed and scattered onto the lawn for all to see. Tiny pink babies with no prickles lay baking in the sun as the heartbroken little mother shuffled from one to another.

Rolly, the self imposed company leader

From his bungalow window the householder viewed the drama with horror before he dashed out to cancel the complete operation. He wouldn't have intentionally unearthed the habitat for all the world and he surveyed the devastation with paralysing guilt. He knew not to touch the babies or the mother would kill or abandon them. So wretchedly he moved away. For two hours he watched a desperate parent carry away six babies by the scruff of their necks, and gather the wreck of her precious home to cover them. Possibly exhaustion, the inability to count or the fact that the seventh baby was now cold and covered in flies prompted the weary mum to leave him behind. The human observer decided that now he must intervene.

By the time Rolly, barely alive, was admitted to Hedgehog Care, the flies' eggs had developed into maggots which had wriggled into any crevice they could to eat the hoglet alive. In firm hands, combs, tweezers, syringe, paint brush and powder were ruthlessly employed in the urgent task of removing all traces of fly strike from eyes, nose, mouth, armpits, feet, tummy and bottom. The process was vital, painful and distressing. Rolly squeaked pitifully. Warm goats' milk and colostrum temporarily soothed and comforted him but when he was tucked into a clean bed he felt lost, desolate and miserable. Rolly missed his cuddly mum desperately and wanted to die now she had gone. He fell into a deep sleep in which he dreamed of the confident steady thump of his mothers heart beat. He was tightly enveloped in secure warmth and snuggled gratefully into the depth of a pre-natal safety. Well rested he nuzzled for milk, his tiny fingers caressing soft skin. He was not aware that he was spread-eagled on a human neck and the pulse and love of a strange creature was willing him to live.

By the time he was weaned, Rolly had spent six to eight weeks nestling and bobbing about inside jumpers. As he clung lovingly to his human transport, his fuzzy face unexpectedly popping out of a polo neck alarmed many an unsuspecting person encountered as he peeped. After each feed he was coaxed to 'toilet' by the gentle stroking of moistened cotton wool or tissue. He smiled, opened his fat little thighs and remembered his mum as he obliged. Truly affectionate he dispelled many a doubt about his kind being undesirable.

With all the attention he had attracted, Rolly had been featured repeatedly on T.V. and his photographs frequently embellished newspapers and magazines. Now an established celebrity, he preferred to remain discreet about his background as an orphan. Better that he was accepted as a war veteran or traffic hero. This way the girls were impressed and the guys admired and acknowledged him politely. Tonight a newly introduced stranger chose to ignore him and instead, circled and dashed on mysterious errands to nowhere. Cautiously Rolly prickled and blew himself as big as he could but still he was nothing compared to the size of Oliver Brown whose prickles were

laid smoothly, showing no sign of consternation. Rolly was possibly jealous, certainly puzzled and just a shade disappointed. He nudged himself into the path of the hastening hedgehog hoping to prompt some reaction. Oliver Brown merely swerved to avoid contact and continued to concentrate on his amazing ritual. Perturbed, Rolly tentatively investigated the new box, scuffed the blankets about then chuckled wickedly as an idea sparked. Hoisting his back legs to their full extent he dropped a very rude parcel in the middle of the bed then wiped his dirty bottom on the sides of the box. "Ignore that!" he thought as he hurriedly made his exit, trundled merrily to a corner and stood by to watch.

Eventually Oliver Brown re-entered his box only to turn abruptly and fall out. Inwardly he was disgusted by what he saw, outwardly he showed no emotion. He ran about for a considerable time and when he was tired he slept openly in the centre of the hearth rub. Rolly didn't like him at all.

Night after night Rolly teased and provoked and became increasingly frustrated and angry at Oliver Brown's indifference. As if ever racing against time Oliver Brown urgently gathered tea-towels, socks, papers and anything available into heaps that he fashioned into cozy resting places, then, as basic instinct eluded him, he slept where he dropped without utilising his efforts. The urge to build was present but the natural drive to protect himself was gone.

Rolly reluctantly recognised the good looks but knew there was something decidedly odd about this fellow. He was infuriating so Rolly paid evil disrespects at every opportunity on every creation that Oliver Brown completed. Insulted by apparent aloofness Rolly's anger exploded, at intervals, into wild tantrums. He snatched hold of Oliver Brown's fluffy skirt below his prickles and shook and shook like a terrier worrying a mop. Forlorn squawks of bewilderment summoned rescue to separate ferocious little Rolly from handsome dignified gentleman, Oliver Brown. He didn't try to contest or understand this funny world. So long as pink fingers didn't take liberties or his dinner wasn't late he was a simple contented and lovable lad.

Resigned to a domesticated indoor life, the handicapped boys took readily to travel and socialising. So delighted were people to meet the famous rivals, face to face, that questions were asked when other hedgehog personalities would take their turn on the rota for attendance at visits and talks. Drawings and letters of thanks from school children always acknowledged their charm but Oliver Brown caused a stir when he 'whoopsied' under the wardrobe during a walk about in a school assembly hall. Thrilled children pinpointed that mishap as the highlight of their talk. He was often invited for return visits because his learning difficulties touched the soft spots of so many hearts. Taped recordings of hedgehog

like a terrier worrying a mop.

songs were beautifully sung by school children and addressed to Oliver Brown. Also inspired by him, as a precious patient, was a Valentine poem written for a competition and won by Hedgehog Care:

> Gone are the passions, the tears and the joys
> Of yesterday's romances, sweethearts and boys
> I remember the letters, the poems, the proses,
> The phone call, the outings, the chocolates, the roses.
> But dearer to me than the prettiest posy
> Is the dew drop that hangs from your little wet nosey.
> Reclusive, elusive, wandering nightly
> Unprickle the charms that you've rolled up so tightly.
> You shy little treasure, I wish you were mine
> I wish you would love me, be my Valentine.
> Please stay here and share my life, don't go away
> Oh wild one, dear Hedgehog, my love of today.

(Only excusable as a last resort, captivity poses many problems, freedom is a birthright essential for health and happiness).

Although dog biscuits and bones were included in the diet to help keep teeth clean, like all long-stay patients Oliver Brown developed dental problems and twice yearly needed the vet to scale his teeth to prevent gingivitis and other related infections. An apparent loss of appetite is often in reality an extremely painful mouth condition which makes eating impossible in spite of ravenous hunger.

One morning poor Oliver Brown was discovered

sleeping in an uncomfortable position with his leg unnaturally behind him. Closer examination revealed that he had caught his toe in a loose nylon strand from the carpet and his consequent frantic circling had entangled and almost amputated the end of his foot. It turned gangrenous entailing weeks of dressings, antibiotics and trips to the vet. A curious little girl in the veterinary centre waiting room asked what was in the carrying box and was most concerned to learn that it was Oliver Brown. She knew him well from his visit to her school. Evidently the news was taken back to class because during the following week the celebrated patient received a deluge of cards, presents and good wishes for a speedy recovery. Could it have been their prayers or hedgehog's determination that helped his withered little toes improve suddenly before healing completely? There was great rejoicing when he resumed his public appearances.

An element of contention ran between the human residents at Hedgehog Care. Two of the men folk were active country sport supporters with controversial opinions. Feelings ran high but argument and reasoning were fruitless so the subject was usually avoided. Everyone was convinced that their own belief was the right one.

When Oliver Brown was in search of nest building material he noticed something useful on the edge of the settee. It was a treasured tweed shooting cap pinned with a Field Sports Badge and just what was needed to form the base of a hedgehog bed. He could just reach it when he stood on tiptoe and a few tugs landed it on to the carpet. From there it was pushed, dragged and carried up and down the untidy floor until the nest site was chosen. A glove, a pillow case and the cover of a magazine were added to the collection. Oliver Brown then proceeded to work the usual comfort into his creation. Expertly he brushed the fabric into a cozy fuzz and as usual fell asleep by the side of it all. The whole procedure was observed in anticipation and amusement by the ever scornful Rolly and when all was still he crept stealthily out to deposit his disgusting message before scuttling away to roll about in merriment. His jubilation hadn't diminished over the years, his well worn habitual smelly prank was enjoyed just as enthusiastically as ever.

The owner of the hat returned, cursed the hedgehog and grabbed his dusty object impatiently. Rolly prickled in alarm at the roar emitted from the human who flung the hat, containing hot moist droppings, out of the window into the rain. Oliver Brown slept on oblivious to the subtle but unintentional protest in which he had silently taken part. Rolly stifled his mirth as he slipped into hiding.

Hedgehog Care fame had spread overseas to the pages of International editorials and waves of radio programmes. Suddenly Canadians and Americans desperately wanted to buy hedgehogs as pets. Endearing as

carried up and down the untidy floor

they might be it is unfair to keep healthy ones captive and they certainly don't belong over there. They are not happy in zoos, pet shops or aquariums with wood shavings – what is more, no human has the right to trade in wild animals. Their dignity, privacy, freedom and habitat should be preserved as birthrights.

In their hospital sanctuary Oliver Brown and prickly company were gradually gathering more and more friends, fans and admirers who wrote, supported and visited from all over the world. The cluttered cottage was becoming so overcrowded that a vague dream of renovating the stables to provide an extra ward for convalescent patients was put into effect. There was a lot of work to be done and the limited staff was already stretched with nursing round the clock. There was no money to pay builders. Family and friends rallied to the cause with time, energy and effort, as well as donations, materials and fittings. It was all very exciting. When help was volunteered from Interskill, a local unit for people with learning difficulties, their labour was gratefully accepted. They worked hard and cheerfully, designing, building and fitting rows of hedgehog cages. They took a break for Christmas and the New Year. And one January morning as work stood still the world itself temporarily stood still at Hedgehog Care. Being in existence for seven years had covered the average lifespan of a hedgehog and some of the originals were showing signs of wear and tear. In the early hours of a winter morning Oliver Brown was called gently home to rest for ever in his Heavenly habitat. Like everyone, Rolly was absolutely devastated, realising only now that his inoffensive sparring partner had given a whole purpose to his life in care. He hadn't been such a bad chap, in fact he missed him already. No more target practice. Sneaky plops and bubbles of laughter were things of the past. Happy memories.

Rolly and the rest of the team were all taken outside to attend the funeral. A pathetic little party of people and handicapped hedgehogs gathered by the grave. Together with Oliver Brown they had worked miracles in public relations. Silently they read the specially composed words on the tombstone spelling hopes for yet another departed friend.

> Goodnight hedgehog
> Loved briefly by few in our weary world
> of mistakes and indifference
> Wake up with hope in your happy heaven
> of grubs and peace and country treasures
> Where roads and poisons and humans
> will never hurt you or your habitat again.
> Amen

Goodnight and thankyou Oliver Brown. There was now a new interest, understanding and awareness of hedgehogs and their problems. A complete change in attitude could

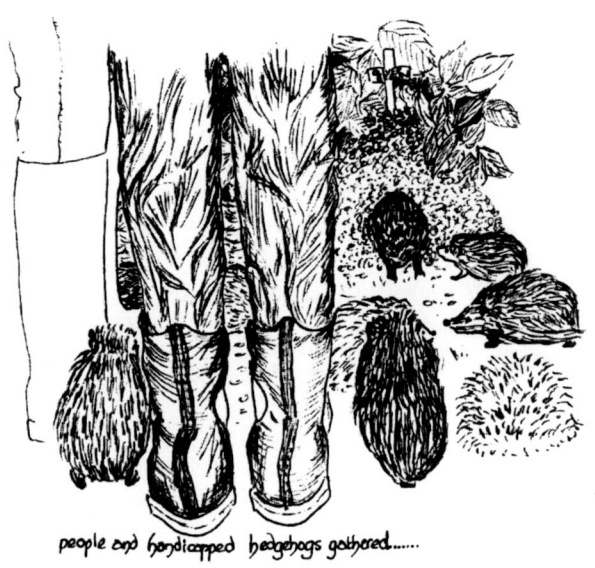

people and handicapped hedgehogs gathered......

only be beneficial to their future welfare. People were even campaigning to bring about new legislation to have the species protected by law.

Rolly hoisted his hind legs high to deliver his usual communication but there was no merriment. Reverent and serious he strained carefully to position his deposit near the crumbly earth that softly covered Oliver Brown. This time it was a salute, a symbol of respect, affection and 'Goodbye for now' to a hedgehog loved my many and admired by Rolly.

Building was resumed, the new yard was completed 'Hogsfam' was installed upstairs, selling donated clothes to raise funds for maintaining lights and heating in the additional unit. In March the dream was achieved and officially opened and celebrated on television at a ceremony attended by the lovely people with learning difficulties from Interskill. It seemed appropriate that their wonderful work should be acknowledged by paying tribute to a special hedgehog who had also triumphed over learning difficulties. People who came from all over the world to visit Hedgehog Care were proudly welcomed to 'THE OLIVER BROWN WARD'. Now he would never be forgotten.

To briefly answer inquiries with "He was a brain damaged hedgehog" couldn't do him justice. Oliver Brown the Hedgehog needed and deserved a book to explain exactly who he was.

he would never be forgotten